ECLECTIC EDUCATIONAL SERIES.

M^CGUFFEY'S

FIRST

ECLECTIC READER.

REVISED EDITION.

NEW YORK ∴ CINCINNATI ∴ CHICAGO

AMERICAN BOOK COMPANY

Suggestions to Teachers.

This FIRST READER may be used in teaching reading by any of the methods in common use; but it is especially adapted to the Phonic Method, the Word Method, or a combination of the two.

I. PHONIC METHOD.—First teach the elementary sounds and their representatives, the letters marked with diacriticals, as they occur in the lessons; then, the formation of words by the combination of these sounds. For instance, teach the pupil to identify the characters ă, ŏ, n, d, ğ, r, and th, in Lesson I, as the representatives of certain elementary sounds; then, teach him to form words by their combination, and to identify them at sight. Use first the words at the head of the lesson, then other words, as, *nag, on, and,* etc. Pursue a similar course in teaching the succeeding lessons. Having read a few lessons in this manner, begin to teach the names of the letters and the spelling of words, and require the groups, " a man," " the man," " a pen," " the pen," to be read as a good reader would pronounce single words.

II. When one of the letters in the combinations *ou* or *ow,* is marked in the words at the head of the reading exercises, the other is silent. If neither is marked, the two letters represent a diphthong. All other unmarked vowels in the vocabularies, when *in combination,* are silent letters. In slate or blackboard work, the silent letters may be canceled.

III. WORD METHOD.—Teach the pupil to identify at sight the words placed at the head of the reading exercises, and to read these exercises without hesitation. Having read a few lessons, begin to teach the names of the letters and the spelling of words.

IV. WORD METHOD AND PHONIC METHOD COMBINED.--Teach the pupil to identify words and read sentences, as above. Having read a few lessons in this manner, begin to use the Phonic Method, combining it with the Word Method, by first teaching the words in each lesson *as words;* then, the elementary sounds, the names of the letters, and spelling.

V. Teach the pupil to use script letters in writing, when teaching the names of the letters and the spelling of words.

M'C IST ED. REV
EF 461

PREFACE.

In presenting McGUFFEY'S REVISED FIRST READER to the public, attention is invited to the following features:

1. Words of only two or three letters are used in the first lessons. Longer and more difficult ones are gradually introduced as the pupil gains aptness in the mastery of words.

2. A proper gradation has been carefully preserved. All new words are placed at the head of each lesson, to be learned before the lesson is read. Their number in the early lessons is very small, thus making the first steps easy. All words in these vocabularies are used in the text immediately following.

3. Carefully engraved script exercises are introduced for a double purpose. These should be used to teach the reading of script; and may also serve as copies in slate work.

4. The illustrations have been designed and engraved specially for the lessons in which they occur. Many of these engravings will serve admirably as the basis for oral lessons in language.

5. The type is large, strong, and distinct.

The credit for this revision is almost wholly due to the many friends of McGUFFEY'S READERS, — eminent teachers and scholars, who have contributed suggestions and criticisms gained from their daily work in the schoolroom.

Cincinnati, June, 1879.

THE ALPHABET.

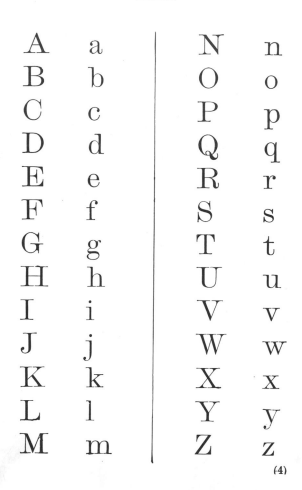

A	a	N	n
B	b	O	o
C	c	P	p
D	d	Q	q
E	e	R	r
F	f	S	s
G	g	T	t
H	h	U	u
I	i	V	v
J	j	W	w
K	k	X	x
L	l	Y	y
M	m	Z	z

Script Alphabet.

SCRIPT FIGURES

1 2 3 4 5 6 7 8 9 0

(vi)

dŏḡ the rǎn

ă ŏ n d ḡ r th

The dog.

The dog ran.

LESSON II.

căt   măt   ĭṣ   ŏn

ȼ   t   ĭ   m   ṣ

The cat.   The mat.

Is the cat on the mat?

The cat is on the mat.

LESSON III.

ĭt	hĭṣ	pĕn	hănd
a	ĭn	hăṣ	măn

p   h   ĕ

The man.   A pen.

The man has a pen.
Is the pen in his hand?
It is in his hand.

LESSON IV.

hĕn
făt
răt
bŏx

bĭḡ   rŭn   frŏm   ĕan

f   b   x   ŭ

A fat hen.   A big rat.

The fat hen is on the box.
The rat ran from the box.
Can the hen run?

LESSON V.

Răb   Ann   hăt   cătch   sēe

ē   ch   s

See Rab! See Ann!
See! Rab has the hat.
Can Ann catch Rab?

LESSON VI.

shē   păt   to͞o   now
lĕt   mē

sh   o͞o   ow   l

Ann can catch Rab.
See! She has the hat.
Now Ann can pat Rab.
Let me pat Rab, too.

LESSON VII.

Nĕd   ĕḡgṣ   blăck   lĕft
fĕd   nĕst   thĕm   ḡĕt

wĭll   a   black   hen   the   nest

w   ck

Ned has fed the hen.

She is a black hen.

She has left the nest.

See the eggs in the nest!

Will the hen let Ned get them?

LESSON VIII.

hĕad　　　　hē　　　　Năt
cŏme　　　　wĭth　　　ănd
　　　　　　ŏ

Let me get the black hat.
Now Ned has it on his head,
and he is a big man.

Come, Nat, see the big man
with his black hat.

LESSON IX. REVIEW.

pat	catch	has	left
hat	can	black	eggs
Rab	Ann	fed	get

Ned is on the box. He has a pen in his hand. A big rat is in the box. Can the dog catch the rat?

Come with me, Ann, and see the man with a black hat on his head.

The fat hen has left the nest. Run, Nat, and get the eggs.

SLATE WORK.

The cat ran. Ann ran. The man has a hat.

LESSON X.

Nĕll	sȯme
păn	hĭm
yĕs	dọ
yọu	hăve
I	tọ

ī   y   v   ọ

Do you see Nell?

Yes; she has a pan with some eggs in it.

Let me have the pan and the eggs, will you, Nell?

Has the black hen left the nest?

I will now run to catch Rab. Will you run, too?

LESSON XI.

O	whĭp	Bĕn
ŭp	stĭll	sĭt
ĭf	stănd	Jĭp

ō   wh   j

O Ben! let me get in, will you?

Yes, if you will sit still.

Stand still, Jip, and let Ann get in.

Now, Ben, hand me the whip.

Get up, Jip!

1, 2.

LESSON XII.

Kĭt′tў
nīçe
swēet
sĭng
jŭst
hăng
cāġe
thĕn

sŏng   pĕt   pṳt   nŏt

k ġ ç ā ў ng ṳ

Kitty has a nice pet. It can
sing a sweet song.

She has just fed it.

She will now put it in the
cage, and hang the cage up.
Then the cat can not catch it.

LESSON XIII.

Tŏm   tŏp   Kĭt′tў′s̱

ăt

băck

lŏŏk

ḡŏŏd   dŏll   thĭṉk   spŏt

th   ṉ   ŏŏ

Look at Tom and his dog. The dog has a black spot on his back. Do you think he is a good dog?

Tom has a big top, too. It is on the box with Kitty's doll.

LESSON XIV.

sŭn	wē	how	pŏnd
stŏp	fôr	ḡō	swĭm
hẽr	ŭs	hŏt	dŭck

ẽ   ô

The sun is up. The man has fed the black hen and the fat duck.

Now the duck will swim in the pond. The hen has run to her nest.

Let us not stop at the pond now, for it is hot.

See how still it is! We will go to see Tom and his top.

LESSON XV.

Jŏhn	rŏck	sĕt	jŭmp
fŭn	mŭst	māy	ŭn′der
skĭp	băn͟k	bŭt	toŭch

O John! the sun has just set. It is not hot, now.

Let us run and jump. I think it is fun to run, and skip, and jump.

See the duck on the pond! Her nest is up on the bank, under the rock.

We must not touch the nest, but we may look at it.

LESSON XVI. REVIEW.

The sun has set, and the pond is still.

John, Ned, Ben, Tom, and Nell stand on the bank, and look at the duck.

The dog with a black spot on his back, is with Tom. See! Tom has his hat in his hand. He has left his big top on the box.

Kitty's doll is on the rock.

Nell has put her pet in the cage. It will sing a sweet song. The duck has her nest under the rock.

It is not hot now. Let us run, and skip, and jump on the bank. Do you not think it is fun?

LESSON XVII.

äre ĭnk mŏss thĭs tŭb up sĕt'
ä

SLATE WORK.

The pen and the ink are on
the stand. Is this a good
pen? The moss is on the
rock. This duck can swim.
Ben upset the tub.

LESSON XVIII.

nŭt dĭd shŭt shăll lŏst fŏx
mĕn mĕt stĕp ĭn'tọ hŭnt mŭd

SLATE WORK.

Will the dog hunt a fox?
Ben lost his hat. Shall I
shut the box? I met him
on the step. Did you jump
into the mud? I have a
nut. I met the men.

LESSON XIX.

Kāte	ōld	nō	ḡràss
dēar	līkes	bē	drĭnk
mĭlk	ꞓow	out	ḡĭveṣ

à

O Kate! the old cow is in the pond: see her drink! Will she not come out to get some grass?

No, John, she likes to be in the pond. See how still she stands!

The dear old cow gives us sweet milk to drink.

LESSON XX.

mam mä′	lärġe	ăṣ	pa pä′
ärmṣ	rīde	fär	bärn
bōth	Prĭnçe	trŏt	yọur

Papa, will you let me ride with you on Prince? I will sit still in your arms.

See, mamma! We are both on Prince. How large he is!

Get up, Prince! You are not too fat to trot as far as the barn.

LESSON XXI.

ŏf (ŏv)	thăt	tŏss	fạll
wĕll	Făn'nў	bạll	wạll
wạṣ	pret'tў (prĭt-)	dòne	whạt
	ạ	ạ	

O Fanny, what a pretty ball!

Yes; can you catch it, Ann?

Toss it to me, and see. I will not let it fall.

That was well done.

Now, Fanny, toss it to the
top of the wall, if you can.

LESSON XXII.

hăd	wĕnt	eạll	mīght
flăḡ	nēar	swăm	swĭng

Did you call us, mamma?

I went with Tom to the pond. I had my doll, and Tom had his flag.

The fat duck swam to the bank, and we fed her. Did you think we might fall into the pond?

We did not go too near, did we, Tom?

May we go to the swing, now, mamma?

LESSON XXIII.

hēre	bănd	hēar	hôrse
plāy	they	pȧss	whêre
frȯnt	fīne	hōpe	çȯmeş

ê   e̱

Here comes the band! Shall we call mamma and Fanny to see it?

Let us stand still, and hear the men play as they pass.

I hope they will stop here and play for us.

See the large man in front of the band, with his big hat. What has he in his hand? How fine he looks!

Look, too, at the man on that fine horse.

If the men do not stop, let us go with them and see where they go.

LESSON XXIV.

Bĕss	hăp'pў	māke	eärt
tĕnt	wŏŏdṣ	lĭt'tle	vĕr'ў
bĕd	Rŏb'ert	ḡŏne	drạw

Bess and Robert are very happy; papa and mamma have gone to the woods with them.

Robert has a big tent and a

flag, and Bess has a little bed for her doll.

Jip is with them. Robert will make him draw Bess and her doll in the cart.

LESSON XXV.

Jāmeṣ · Mā′rў

māde · săng

mӯ · lay

spōrt · spāde

lăp · dĭḡ

dŏll'ṣ · sănd

said (sĕd) · ӯ

"Kate, will you play with me?"

said James. "We will dig in the sand with this little spade. That will be fine sport."

"Not now, James," said Kate; "for I must make my doll's bed. Get Mary to play with you."

James went to get Mary to play with him. Then Kate made the doll's bed.

She sang a song to her doll, and the doll lay very still in her lap.

Did the doll hear Kate sing?

LESSON XXVI.

ĭts	shāde	broŏk	pĭcks	ạll
bȳ	hĕlp	stōneṣ	ḡlăd	sŏft

Kate has left her doll in its little bed, and has gone to play

with Mary and James. They are all in the shade, now, by the brook.

James digs in the soft sand with his spade, and Mary picks up little stones and puts them in her lap.

James and Mary are glad to see Kate. She will help them pick up stones and dig, by the little brook.

1, 3.

LESSON XXVII. REVIEW

"What shall we do?" said Fanny to John. "I do not like to sit still. Shall we hunt for eggs in the barn?"

"No," said John; "I like to play on the grass. Will not papa let us catch Prince, and go to the big woods?

"We can put the tent in the cart, and go to some nice spot where the grass is soft and sweet."

"That will be fine," said Fanny. "I will get my doll, and give her a ride with us."

"Yes," said John, "and we will get mamma to go, too. She will hang up a swing for us in the shade."

LESSON XXVIII.

pēep   whīle
tāke   slēep

tŭck   sāfe   ōh   wĕt   fēet
chĭck   ċan't   fēelṣ   wĭng

Peep, peep! Where have you gone, little chick? Are you lost? Can't you get back to the hen?

Oh, here you are! I will take you back. Here, hen, take this little chick under your wing.

Now, chick, tuck your little,

wet feet under you, and go to sleep for a while.

Peep, peep! How safe the lit-tle chick feels now!

LESSON XXIX.

wĭnd	tīme	thêre	fĕnçe
kīte	hīgh	eȳeṣ	brĭght
flieṣ	whȳ	dāy	shīneṣ

This is a fine day. The sun shines bright. There is a good wind, and my kite flies high. I can just see it.

The sun shines in my eyes; I will stand in the shade of this high fence.

Why, here comes my dog! He was under the cart. Did you see him there?

What a good time we have had! Are you not glad that we did not go to the woods with John?

SLATE WORK.

The pond is still. How it shines in the hot sun! Let us go into the woods where we can sit in the shade.

LESSON XXX.

wĭsh	flōat	tīe	knōw
rōpe	bōat	trȳ	shōre
gĭvc	pōle	dōn't	pu̇sh
drăḡ	wōn't	ōar	fŭn'nȳ

"Kate, I wish we had a boat to put the dolls in. Don't you?"

"I know what we can do. We can get the little tub, and tie a rope to it, and drag it to the pond. This will float with the dolls in it, and we can get a pole to push it from the shore."

"What a funny boat, Kate! A tub for a boat, and a pole for an oar! Won't it upset?"

"We can try it, Nell, and see."

"Well, you get the tub, and I will get a pole and a rope. We will put both dolls in the tub, and give them a ride."

SLATE WORK.

The dolls had a nice ride to the pond. A soft wind made the tub float out. Nell let the pole fall on the tub, and upset it.

LESSON XXXI.

| bound | Rōṣe | called | g̅ŏt |
| drown | found | brāve | cāme |

| Pŏn′tō | jŭmped | mouth |
| a round′ | brôught | wạ′ter |

"Here, Ponto! Here, Ponto!" Kate called to her dog. "Come, and get the dolls out of the pond."

Rose went under, but she did not drown. Bess was still on the top of the water.

Ponto came with a bound, and jumped into the pond. He swam around, and got Bess in his mouth, and brought her to the shore.

Ponto then found Rose, and brought her out, too.

Kate said, "Good, old Ponto! Brave old dog!"

What do you think of Ponto?

LESSON XXXII.

Jūne	Lū′çў′ș	âir	kīnd
trēeș	sĭng′ing	blūe	whĕn
pūre	sayș (sĕz)	skȳ	pĭe′nĭe

ū   â

What a bright June day!
The air is pure. The sky is
as blue as it can be.

Lucy and her mamma are in
the woods. They have found a
nice spot, where there is some
grass.

They sit in the shade of the
trees, and Lucy is singing.

The trees are not large, but they make a good shade.

Lucy's kind mamma says that they will have a picnic when her papa can get a tent.

LESSON XXXIII. REVIEW.

James and Robert have gone into the shade of a high wall to play ball.

Mary and Lucy have come up from the pond near by, with brave old Ponto, to see them play.

When they toss the ball up in the air, and try to catch it, Ponto runs to get it in his mouth.

Now the ball is lost. They all look for it under the trees

and in the grass; but they can not see it. Where can it be?

See! Ponto has found it. Here he comes with it. He will lay it at little Lucy's feet, or put it in her hand.

LESSON XXXIV.

boy	our	spoil	hụr räh′
ōwn	coil	noiṣe	fo͞urth
sŭch	join	thăṉk	a bout′
hoist	pāy	Ju lȳ′	plāy′ing
		oi	

"Papa, may we have the big flag?" said James.

"What can my little boy do with such a big flag?"

"Hoist it on our tent, papa. We are playing Fourth of July."

"Is that what all this noise

is about? Why not hoist your own flags?"

"Oh! they are too little."

"You might spoil my flag."

"Then we will all join to pay for it. But we will not spoil it, papa."

"Take it, then, and take the coil of rope with it."

"Oh! thank you. Hurrah for the flag, boys!"

LESSON XXXV.

fĭn′ished   bŏn′net   lĕs′son

sāved   whīte

a wāy′   I′ve

ăm   wõrk

seăm′per   rĕad′ў   gär′den

THE WHITE KITTEN.

Kitty, my pretty, white kitty,
   Why do you scamper away?
I've finished my work and my lesson,
   And now I am ready for play.

Come, kitty, my own little kitty,
   I've saved you some milk come and see;
Now drink while I put on my bonnet,
   And play in the garden with me.

eâre	ạl'wāyṣ	līne	Frănk
rōw	been (bĭn)	kēeps	hōme

Frank has a pretty boat. It is white, with a black line near the water.

He keeps it in the pond, near his home. He always takes good care of it.

Frank has been at work in the garden, and will now row a while.

LESSON XXXVII.

mŭch	one (wŭn)	yĕt	hŭn͟'ḡrў
sēen	ḡrănd'mä	çôrn	wọuld

ọ

"What is that?" said Lucy, as she came out on the steps. "Oh, it is a little boat! What a pretty one it is!"

"I will give it to you when it is finished," said John, kindly. "Would you like to have it?"

"Yes, very much, thank you, John. Has grandma seen it?"

"Not yet; we will take it to her by and by. What have you in your pan, Lucy?"

"Some corn for my hens, John; they must be very hungry by this time."

1, 4.

LESSON XXXVIII.

mär′ket   brĕad

bȧs′ket   bôught

mēat

tēa

trȳ′ing

tĕll

whĭch

James has been to market with his mamma.

She has bought some bread, some meat, and some tea, which are in the basket on her arm.

James is trying to tell his mamma what he has seen in the market.

LESSON XXXIX.

rēads̩	sō	weârs̩	plēas̩e
eọuld	hâir		
fȧst	lȯve		
ēas̩′y̆	ḡrāy		
châir	whọ		

ḡlȧss′es̩

See my dear, old grandma in her easy-chair! How gray her hair is! She wears glasses when she reads.

She is always kind, and takes such good care of me that I like to do what she tells me.

When she says, "Robert, will you get me a drink?" I run as fast as I can to get it for her. Then she says, "Thank you, my boy."

Would you not love a dear, good grandma, who is so kind? And would you not do all you could to please her?

LESSON XL.

dȯeṣ	wȯn′der	mȯth′er	ȯth′er
bēe	hȯn′ĕȳ	lĭs′ten	flow′er

"Come here, Lucy, and listen! What is in this flower?"

"O mother! it is a bee. I wonder how it came to be shut up in the flower!"

"It went into the flower for

some honey, and it may be it went to sleep. Then the flower shut it in.

"The bee likes honey as well as we do, but it does not like to be shut up in the flower.

"Shall we let it out, Lucy?"

"Yes; then it can go to other flowers, and get honey."

LESSON XLI.

bĕst	hĭtched	thêir	shǫuld
ôr	rīd′ing	lĭve	hōlds̠
hāy	drīv′ing	tīght	ẽar′lў

Here come Frank and James White. Do you know where they live?

Frank is riding a horse, and James is driving one hitched to a cart. They are out very early in the day. How happy they are!

See how well Frank rides, and how tight James holds the lines!

The boys should be kind to their horses. It is not best to whip them.

When they have done riding, they will give the horses some hay or corn.

SLATE WORK.

Some horses can trot very fast. Would you like to ride fast? One day I saw a dog hitched to a little cart. The cart had some corn in it.

LESSON XLII.

lŏŏk'ing　　　　thôught　　　　pĭck'ing

hẽard　　　　　　　　　　　　　chĭrp

wẽre　　　　　　　　　　　　　tōld

sẽarch　　　　　　　　　　　　dēar'lў

yoŭng　　　　　　　　　　　　ḡĩrl

lȯved　　　　　　　　　　　　bĭrds̤

chĭl'dren　　　　　　be sīdes̤'

A little girl went in search
of flowers for her mother. It
was early in the day, and the
grass was wet. Sweet little birds
were singing all around her.

And what do you think she
found besides flowers? A nest
with young birds in it.

While she was looking at

them, she heard the mother
bird chirp, as if she said, "Do
not touch my children, little girl,
for I love them dearly."

The little girl now thought
how dearly her own mother
loved her.

So she left the birds. Then,
picking some flowers, she went
home, and told her mother what
she had seen and heard.

LESSON XLIII.

eight	ȧsk	ȧft′er	town
pȧst	äh	tĭck′et	rīght
hälf	twọ	trāin	dĭng
	lĭght′ning		

"Mamma, will you go to town?"

"What do you ask for a ticket
on your train?"

"Oh! we will give you a ticket, mamma."

"About what time will you get back?"

"At half past eight."

"Ah! that is after bedtime. Is this the fast train?"

"Yes, this is the lightning train."

"Oh! that is too fast for me."

"What shall we get for you in town, mamma?"

"A big basket, with two good little children in it."

"All right! Time is up! Ding, ding!"

LESSON XLIV.

scho͞ol	ē′ven (ē′vn)	thrēe
ro͞om		smạll

bŏok	tēach′er	no͞on
rụde	rēad′ing	po͞or

It is noon, and the school is out. Do you see the children

at play? Some run and jump, some play ball, and three little girls play school under a tree.

What a big room for such a small school!

Mary is the teacher. They all have books in their hands, and Fanny is reading.

They are all good girls, and would not be rude even in playing school.

Kate and Mary listen to Fanny as she reads from her book.

What do you think she is reading about? I will tell you. It is about a poor little boy who was lost in the woods.

When Fanny has finished, the three girls will go home.

In a little while, too, the boys will give up their playing.

LESSON XLV.

ăp′ple	mew	tēaṣe	cṛăck′er
down	new	sĭl′lў	a slēep′
wąnts	cąllṣ	knew	friĕndṣ
up ŏn′	flew	Pŏll	Pŏl′lў

Lucy has a new pet. Do you know what kind of bird it is? Lucy calls her Polly.

Polly can say, "Poor Poll! Poor

Poll! Polly wants a cracker;" and she can mew like a cat.

But Polly and the cat are not good friends. One day Polly flew down, and lit upon the cat's back when she was asleep.

I think she knew the cat would not like that, and she did it to tease her.

When Lucy pets the cat, Polly flies up into the old apple tree, and will not come when she calls her. Then Lucy says, "What a silly bird!"

LESSON XLVI. Review.

"Well, children, did you have a nice time in the woods?"

"Oh yes, mother, such a good time! See what sweet flowers

we found, and what soft moss.
The best flowers are for grandma. Won't they please her?"

"Yes; and it will please grandma to know that you thought of
her."

"Rab was such a
good dog, mother.

We left him under the big tree
by the brook, to take care of
the dolls and the basket.

"When we came back, they
were all safe. No one could
get them while Rab was there.

We gave him some of the crackers from the basket.

"O mother, how the birds did sing in the woods!

"Fanny said she would like to be a bird, and have a nest in a tree. But I think she would want to come home to sleep."

"If she were a bird, her nest would be her home. But what would mother do, I wonder, without her little Fanny?"

LESSON XLVII.

bēach	shĕlls	thēṣe	sēat
wāveṣ	gō'ing	ĕv'er	sêa
watch	ē'ven ing	lā'zy̆	sīde

These boys and girls live near the sea. They have been to the

beach. It is now evening, and they are going home.

John, who sits on the front seat, found some pretty shells. They are in the basket by his side.

Ben White is driving. He holds the lines in one hand, and his whip in the other.

1. 5

Robert has his hat in his hand, and is looking at the horses. He thinks they are very lazy; they do not trot fast.

The children are not far from home. In a little while the sun will set, and it will be bedtime.

Have you ever been at the seaside? Is it not good sport to watch the big waves, and to play on the wet sand?

LESSON XLVIII.

lŏḡ	quī′et	proud	puॢlled
fĭsh	stŭmp	rĭv′er	fä′ther

One evening Frank's father said to him, "Frank, would you like to go with me to catch some fish?"

"Yes; may I go? and with you, father?"

"Yes, Frank, with me."

"Oh, how glad I am!"

Here they are, on the bank of a river. Frank has just pulled a fine fish out of the water. How proud he feels!

See what a nice, quiet spot they have found. Frank has the stump of a big tree for his seat, and his father sits on a log near by. They like the sport.

LESSON XLIX.

rāin	out'sīde	ŏf'ten	pĭt'ter
sāy	wĭn'dow	sound	păt'ter
drŏps	sòme'tīmeṣ	ōn'lў	mū'ṣie

SLATE WORK.

I wish, Mamma you would tell me where the rain comes from. Does it come from the sky? And when the little drops pitter-patter on the window do you think they are playing with me? I can not work or read, for I love to listen to them. I often think their sound is pretty music. But the rain keeps children at home and sometimes I do not like that; then,

The little raindrops only say,
"Pit, pitter, patter, pat;
While <u>we</u> play on the <u>out</u>-side,
Why can't <u>you</u> play on that?"

LESSON L.

slĕd	thrōw	wĭn′ter	hûrt
içe	cŏv′er	Hĕn′rў	nĕxt
skāte	ḡround	mĕr′rў	snōw
sĭs′ter	läugh′ing (läf′ing)		pâir

I like winter, when snow and ice cover the ground. What fun it is to throw snowballs, and to skate on the ice!

See the boys and girls! How merry they are! Henry has his sled, and draws his little sister. There they go!

I think Henry is kind, for his sister is too small to skate.

Look! Did you see that boy fall down? But I see he is not hurt, for he is laughing.

Some other boys have just come to join in the sport. See them put on their skates.

Henry says, that he hopes his father will get a pair of skates for his sister next winter.

LESSON LI.

pạw   po līte′

mēanṣ   iṣ n't

spēak   sīr

shāke   Fī′dō

trĭcks   tēach

    dĭn′ner

    El′len

    bow′wow

Ellen, do look at Fido! He sits up in a chair, with my hat on. He looks like a little boy; but it is only Fido.

Now see him shake hands. Give me your paw, Fido. How do you do, sir? Will you take dinner with us, Fido? Speak!

Fido says, "Bowwow," which means, "Thank you, I will."

Isn't Fido a good dog, Ellen? He is always so polite.

When school is out, I will try to teach him some other tricks.

LESSON LII.

pŭss　　shĕd
pāin　　wāy
stōle　　saw
hĭd　　ēat

Hăt′tie

sŭf′fer

sŏr′rў

some′thing　　eaught　　trīed　　Nē′rō

"O Hattie!　I just saw a large

rat in the shed; and old Nero tried to catch it."

"Did he catch it, Frank?"

"No, Nero did not; but the old cat did."

"My cat?"

"No, it was the other one."

"Do tell me how she got it, Frank. Did she run after it?"

"No, that was not the way. Puss was hid on a big box. The rat stole out, and she jumped at it and caught it."

"Poor rat! It must have been very hungry; it came out to get something to eat."

"Why, Hattie, you are not sorry puss got the rat, are you?"

"No, I can not say I am sorry she got it; but I do not like to see even a rat suffer pain."

LESSON LIII.

rōll	buĭld	ḡrănd'pä	härd
fōam	shĭps	houṣ'eṣ	lŏng
sāil	breāk	wŏŏd'en	blōw

Mary and Lucy have come down to the beach with their grandpa. They live in a town near the sea.

Their grandpa likes to sit on the large rock, and watch the big ships as they sail far away on the blue sea. Sometimes he sits there all day long.

The little girls like to dig in the sand, and pick up pretty shells. They watch the waves as they roll up on the beach, and break into white foam.

They sometimes make little

houses of sand, and build walls around them; and they dig wells with their small wooden spades.

They have been picking up shells for their little sister. She is too young to come to the beach.

I think all children like to play by the seaside when the sun is bright, and the wind does not blow too hard.

LESSON LIV.

àsked

fōur

nīght

lăd

çĕnts

fĭf'tӯ

wạnt'ed

Wĭl'lie'ṣ

răb'bits

eăr'ried

tĕll'ing

màs'ter

One day, Willie's father saw a boy at the market with four little white rabbits in a basket.

He thought these would be nice pets for Willie; so he asked the lad how much he wanted for his rabbits.

The boy said, "Only fifty cents, sir."

Willie's father bought them, and carried them home.

Here you see the rabbits and their little master. He has a pen for them, and always shuts them in it at night to keep them safe.

He gives them bread and grass to eat. They like grass, and will take it from his hand. He has called in a little friend to see them.

Willie is telling him about their funny ways.

SLATE WORK.

Some rabbits are as white as snow, some are black, and others have white and black spots. What soft, kind eyes they have!

LESSON LV.

bush	eŭn′ning	plāçe	shōw
find	brō′ken	ō′ver	brĭng

a͞gain′ (a͞gĕn′)   fås′ten (fås′n)

"Come here, Rose. Look down into this bush."

"O Willie! a bird's nest! What

cunning, little eggs! May we take it, and show it to mother?"

"What would the old bird do, Rose, if she should come back and not find her nest?"

"Oh, we would bring it right back, Willie!"

"Yes; but we could not fasten it in its place again. If the wind should blow it over, the eggs would get broken."

LESSON LVI.

strŏng   round   drȳ   bĭll   wõrked
sĕndṣ   claẉṣ   flĭt   Gŏd   sprĭng

"How does the bird make the nest so strong, Willie?"

"The mother bird has her bill and her claws to work with, but she would not know how to make the nest if God did not teach her. Do you see what it is made of?"

"Yes, Willie, I see some horse-hairs and some dry grass. The old bird must have worked hard to find all the hairs, and make them into such a pretty, round nest."

"Shall we take the nest, Rose?"

"Oh no, Willie! We must not take it; but we will come and look at it again, some time."

SLATE WORK.

God made the little birds to sing.
And flit from tree to tree;
'Tis He who sends them in the spring
To sing for you and me.

LESSON LVII.

fĕath′erṣ	a gō′	flȳ	wõrm	erŭmb
fēed′ing	ŭg′lў	ŏff	fēed	brown
ḡuĕss				thĭngṣ

"Willie, when I was feeding the birds just now, a little brown bird flew away with a crumb in its bill."

1, 6.

"Where did it go, Rose?"

"I don't know; away off, some-where."

"I can guess where, Rose. Don't you know the nest we saw some days ago? What do you think is in it now?"

"O Willie, I know! Some little brown birds. Let us go and see them."

"All right; but we must not go too near. There! I just saw the old bird fly out of the bush. Stand here, Rose. Can you see?"

"Why, Willie, what ugly little things! What big mouths they have, and no feathers!"

"Keep still, Rose. Here comes the old bird with a worm in her bill. How hard she must work to feed them all!"

LESSON LVIII.

f̣all'ing	counts	wōeṣ	nīgh
be ḡŭn'	ḡriēfs	stärṣ	tēar
môrn'ing	Lôrd	ēach	joyṣ

When the stars at set of sun
   Watch you from on high,
When the morning has begun,
   Think the Lord is nigh.

All you do and all you say,
   He can see and hear:
When you work and when you play,
   Think the Lord is near.

All your joys and griefs He knows,
   Counts each falling tear,
When to Him you tell your woes,
   Know the Lord will hear.

LESSON LIX.

whĭs′tle (whĭs′l)

pŏck′et   wĭl′low

nōte	fĭlled	dĕad	sĭck
wạlk	ĕv′er y̆	blew	lāne
lāme	tāk′ing	eāne	tŏŏk

One day, when Mary was taking a walk down the lane, trying to sing her doll to sleep,

she met Frank, with his basket and cane.

Frank was a poor, little, lame boy. His father and mother were dead. His dear, old grandma took care of him, and tried to make him happy.

Every day, Mary's mother filled Frank's basket with bread and meat, and a little tea for his grandma.

"How do you do, Frank?" said Mary. "Don't make a noise; my doll is going to sleep. It is just a little sick to-day."

"Well, then, let us whistle it to sleep." And Frank, taking a willow whistle out of his pocket, blew a long note.

"Oh, how sweet!" cried Mary. "Do let me try."

LESSON LX.

tûrned	fāçe	erīed	lōw
al'mōst	so͞on	mōre	erȳ
	onçe (wŭns)	be eauṣe'	

"Yes, Mary, I will give it to you, because you are so good to my grandma."

"Oh! thank you very much." Mary blew and blew a long time. "I can't make it whistle," said she, almost ready to cry.

"Sometimes they will whistle, and sometimes they won't," said Frank. "Try again, Mary."

She tried once more, and the whistle made a low, sweet sound. "It whistles!" she cried.

In her joy, she had turned the doll's face down, and its eyes

shut tight, as if it had gone to sleep.

"There!" cried Frank, "I told you the way to put a doll to sleep, is to whistle to it."

"So it is," said Mary. "Dear, little thing; it must be put in its bed now."

So they went into the house. Frank's basket was soon filled, and he went home happy.

LESSON LXI.

stŏŏd	hĭm sĕlf′	flăp′ping	fĭrst
twĕlve	flăpped	wạlked	flăp
o bẹy′	bĕt′ter	Chĭp′pȳ	fōŏd
stōne	be fōre′	chĭck′ens̬	kĕpt

There was once a big, white
hen that had twelve little chickens. They were very small, and

the old hen took good care of them. She found food for them in the daytime, and at night kept them under her wings.

One day, this old hen took her chickens down to a small brook. She thought the air from the water would do them good.

When they got to the brook, they walked on the bank a little while. It was very pretty on the other side of the brook, and the old hen thought she would take her children over there.

There was a large stone in the brook: she thought it would be easy for them to jump to that stone, and from it to the other side.

So she jumped to the stone, and told the children to come after her. For the first time, she found that they would not obey her.

She flapped her wings, and cried, "Come here, all of you! Jump upon this stone, as I did. We can then jump to the other side. Come, now!"

"O mother! we can't, we can't, we can't!" said all the little chickens.

"Yes you can, if you try," said the old hen. "Just flap your wings, as I did, and you can jump over."

"I am flapping my wings," said Chippy, who stood by himself; "but I can't jump any better than I could before."

LESSON LXII.

chīrped   nĕv′er   in dēed′
slōw′lў   rē′al lў
brōod   be ḡăn′
dĭd n't
ūse
dōor
bīte
piēçe

"I never saw such children," said the old hen. "You don't try at all."

"We can't jump so far, mother. Indeed we can't, we can't!" chirped the little chickens.

"Well," said the old hen, "I must give it up." So she jumped back to the bank, and walked slowly home with her brood.

"I think mother asked too much of us," said one little chicken to the others.

"Well, I tried," said Chippy.

"We didn't," said the others; "it was of no use to try."

When they got home, the old hen began to look about for something to eat. She soon found, near the back door, a piece of bread.

So she called the chickens, and they all ran up to her, each one trying to get a bite at the piece of bread.

"No, no!" said the old hen. "This bread is for Chippy. He is the only one of my children that really tried to jump to the stone."

LESSON LXIII.

làst   slātes   wrīte   wāste

nēat   tāk′en   elēan   lẽarn

rēad′er   pâr′ents   sĕe′ond

We have come to the last lesson in this book. We have finished the First Reader.

You can now read all the lessons in it, and can write them on your slates.

Have you taken good care of your book? Children should always keep their books neat and clean.

Are you not glad to be ready for a new book?

Your parents are very kind to send you to school. If you are good, and if you try to learn, your teacher will love you, and you will please your parents.

Be kind to all, and do not waste your time in school.

When you go home, you may ask your parents to get you a Second Reader.

PHONIC CHART.

LONG VOCALS.

ā,	as in	āte.	ẽ,	as in	ẽrr.
â,	"	eâre.	ī,	"	īçe.
ä,	"	ärm.	ō,	"	ōde.
ȧ,	"	lȧst.	ū,	"	ūse.
a̤,	"	a̤ll.	û,	"	bûrn.
ē,	"	ēve.	o͞o,	"	fo͞ol.

SHORT VOCALS.

ă,	as in	ăm.	ŏ,	as in	ŏdd.
ĕ,	"	ĕnd.	ŭ,	"	ŭp.
ĭ,	"	ĭn.	o̬o̬,	"	lo̬o̬k.

DIPHTHONGS.

oi, oy, as in oil, boy. | ou, ow, as in out, now,

ASPIRATES.

f,	as in	fīfe.	t,	as in	tăt.
h,	"	hĭm.	sh,	"	shē,
k,	"	kīte.	ch,	"	chăt.
p,	"	pīpe.	th,	"	thĭck.
s,	"	sāme.	wh,	"	whȳ.

SUBVOCALS.

b,	as in	bĭb.	v,	as in	vălve.
d,	"	dĭd.	th,	"	thĭs.
g,	"	ḡĭḡ.	z,	"	zĭne.
j,	"	jŭḡ.	z,	"	ăzure.
n,	"	nīne.	r,	"	râre.
m,	"	māim.	w,	"	wē.
ng,	"	hăng.	y,	"	yĕt.

l, as in lŭll.

SUBSTITUTES.

ạ, for ŏ, as in whạt.   y̆, for ĭ, as in my̆th.

ê, " â, " thêre.   e, " k, " eăn.

e, " ā, " feint.   ç, " s, " çīte.

ï, " ē, " polïçe.   çh, " sh, " çhāise.

ĩ, " ẽ, " sĩr.   eh, " k, " ehāos.

ȯ, " ŭ, " sȯn.   ġ, " j, " ġĕm.

o, " ōō, " tọ.   n, " ng, " ĭnk.

ọ, " ŏŏ, " wọlf.   ṣ, " z, " ăṣ.

ô, " ạ, " fôrk.   s, " sh, " sure.

õ, " ŭ, " wõrk.   x, " ḡz, " exăet.

ụ, " ŏŏ, " fụll.   gh, " f, " läugh.

ụ, " ōō, " rụde.   ph, " f, " phlŏx.

ȳ, " ī, " flȳ.   qu, " k, " pïque.

qu, for kw, as in quĭt.